17

Poems for a Pandemic
Essays for Quarantine

Copyright © 2020 by Lisa Van Ahn.

All rights reserved. No part of this publication may be reproduced, distributed or transmitted in any form or by any means, including photocopying, recording, or other electronic or mechanical methods, without the prior written permission of the publisher, except in the case of brief quotations embodied in critical reviews and certain other noncommercial uses permitted by copyright law. For permission requests, write to the publisher, addressed "Attention: Permissions Coordinator," at the address below.

LVA Wellness
5136 Hiawatha Ave. S. #1
Minneapolis, MN. 55417

Ordering Information:
Quantity sales. Special discounts are available on quantity purchases by corporations, associations, and others. For details, contact the "Special Sales Department" at the address above.

17- Poems for a Pandemic Essays for Quarantine/—1st ed.

ISBN: 978-1-953449-09-2

DEDICATION

Only if it matters to you, I love you.
Until the end.

A NOTE FROM THE AUTHOR

Wherever you are when you're reading this, and whatever time in the world it is I think it's important for you to know I wrote most of this collection while living through the 2020 Covid 19 pandemic quarantine.

It's the beginning of Spring here in Minneapolis. Everything's ready to blossom, but today the snow is coming down fast and fierce, and it feels like the blossoming is so very far away.

Life is on lock down right now and I've taken to writing to fill my hours and release my emotional frustrations. Much of what's included here has been written in the past 3 weeks and carries a unique perspective on my life in this space,

A few of the pieces pre-date the outbreak.

However, I don't believe in happenstance. All of the works of poetry & essays (both fiction and real life) included in this collecton were meant to live right here. And so they do.

I'm sharing a bit of my world with you via these words, and I hope it helps you feel less alone, or maybe it makes you feel more alone. No matter what, I hope it helps you feel.

Please know this. The sun will come out again. We'll hug long and hard and for sure to the left. Heart to heart.

Until we don't. At some point the hugs will get shorter. We'll forget about the heart to heart connection. We will move easily past each other. Likely, looking down as we mostly did before, because that's just comfortable. We'll reserve our compliments and hold them in our thoughts instead of speaking them out loud, because that's just comfortable. We'll gap from the people we love and get weird about sharing all of ourselves unconditionally, because that's just comfortable.

And when you're ready to be uncomfortable again, remember this: You always can. You always can live a fierce, unapologetic life, and do whatever the hell you want to do. And hopefully that includes loving wildly and feeling all the things. If it doesn't, that's okay too.

xx, LVA-

Table of Contents

PANDEMIC POEMS:

BLACK & WHITE

STAY WITH ME

A NEED FOR VALIDATION

NUNDAY…AGAIN

LAST BREATH

UNTIL THE END

EVERYTHING IS BACKWARDS

A ROAD TRIP

SIX TO TEN

WHEN YOU VENTURE OUT

HEAVY VS. LIGHT

NEW LIFE

WHOLE 30 WHOLE HEARTED

START RIGHT NOW

HOW MUCH

SOME DAYS

THE GREAT STATE OF BEING

QUARANTINE ESSAYS

WASH YOUR HANDS

IT BEGINS WITH A FEVER

WHEN SHE JUMPED

AN ABORTION STORY

PERSPECTIVE

JUST A NUMBER

THE PILL WORKS IF YOU TAKE IT

NINE YEARS OLD

BEGIN AGAIN

ROSIE

ATTACHED

THE CONTAINER

ELLA DIES

A WISH FOR A SCAR

THE ENORMITY OF LIFE

A LOVE LETTER

BECAUSE OF WINTER

ABOUT THE AUTHOR

BLACK & WHITE

It's one or the other, never both
Unless it is
Unless you want black and white
And you appreciate them both
Without needing to blend them to grey
Without needing to say one is right the other wrong
And you appreciate them both
When you see the snow falling bright and white
When you see the cars drive fast turning it to dark black slush
And you appreciate them both
For contrast

STAY WITH ME

When I feel the rising
It's uncomfortable
There's judgement
I'm not doing it well
I'm not enough
There's pain
And there's suffering
One of them is optional
There's judgement
I could do this better
I'm not measuring up
There's the world's point of view
And there's my point of view
One of them is optional
There's judgement
Others aren't doing it right
Others aren't deserving
Both of them are optional
There's judgement
There's also
Acceptance
Forgiveness
Growth
Love
Stay with me
When you feel the rising
In the discomfort
Is a more skillful way to live

Lisa Van Ahn

A NEED FOR VALIDATION

They never loved you
Waiting for your next words
Your thoughts written
To make them feel better about their life
The one they weren't really living
Just scrolling
For a feeling
Something to spark
Excitement. Engagement. Emotions.
And did you love you
Waiting for their likes
On your words written
To make you feel better about your life
The one you were living
So they could scroll
Those feelings
Excitement. Engagement. Emotions.
Wanting to spark the same thing for yourself
A like. A heart. A comment.
Waiting for validation
From anyone other than yourself
You're not good enough to do it on your own
Not enough to love yourself
You need something else or someone else
To believe
You're enough
And it's a small blip on the screen
To make you mean something
A heart that says you matter
Even though
They never loved you

Sequestre Perspective

NUNDAY...AGAIN

Things to say
Never felt this way
Gapping is better
It's safer today
To parcel the story
Of heartache
The one you're
Still telling
Again & Again
It's where you live
Again & Again
Tomorrow is better
Except when it's not
Another Nunday
Or maybe Monday
Feeling like you lost
Your heart
In a moment, of words
On a screen
And it's late on a Sunday
With more words
On a screen
Going nowhere
Or worse, slipping you
Into reverse
You can always try
Again tomorrow
What day is it
Oh right, Nunday again.

Lisa Van Ahn

LAST BREATH

You live your life as it is
Hopefully you hope
For more
Than before
A new awareness
Of yourself
A skill you gained
In seeing the world
With new eyes
You didn't have yesterday
And into your tomorrow
You dream of something
You're creating right now
In this moment
An awareness
That's happening
In the present
And you're Magically
Out of thin air
Manifesting
Just that thing
It's brilliant
Beautiful
Burgeoning
On bliss
Pen to words
And yet what's important to
Write down on paper
Doesn't matter
It's the living that does

Sequestre Perspective

And that happens
Every moment
Until it stops
Until then
Until the end
The last word
Is your last breath
Let it be love

Lisa Van Ahn

UNTIL THE END

Only bringing my heart
I bring that to everything
And it's gonna be brilliant
She said to herself
It was, fact
Actually better than
More like magic
Inexplicable
In one breath
Before pandemic
They met, where
The wild meet
Before the feeding
Frenzy
There's a calm
An opened door
A wrong seat appropriated
A brush on the hand
That hand
The one
It moves across her body
So well now
Like the moment
Happened years ago
Not weeks
Previous to
The silence in the shops
The distancing in the streets
The closing of the country
And still

Sequestre Perspective

They are closer
Than before it all
Which was yesterday
She's always said
Until then
Forever she's said it
Until then to him
And the others
And all of them
She knows better, silly
It doesn't last
Life is brief
A breath in
A breath out
A chance
A small walk
To the river and back
Then it's over
Until then is a fair
And a good thing to say
It's always been
Until now
When all she really wants
To say is
Until the end

Lisa Van Ahn

EVERYTHING IS BACKWARDS

Today I had nothing to do
And don't try to tell me that
There's lots to do everyday
If you really examine it
This world is a pretty bleak place
To create change
Hate is there
Even if you do
Get outside
You can't really
Reciprocity means nothing
It's not true
It's all in our heart
We're all separate, and
I'm sure you understand
My experience
Generates
My attitude
It's all beyond my jurisdiction
In this world of what's happening now
And I'll never believe
Today I had something to do

NOW READ IT IN REVERSE FOR A DIFFERENT P.O.V.

Sequestre Perspective

A ROAD TRIP

Breath rising and falling
One breath
Life rising and falling
One life
Hills rising and falling
One bike
Past rising and falling
One Road trip
It's all the same
And so different
One girl's heart
Rising and falling
One dog's tail
Rising and falling
One anticipation
Rising and falling
One excitement
Rising and falling
One road trip
It's all the same
And so different

Lisa Van Ahn

SIX TO TEN

Paid parking
From six to ten
You're later so it's free
Though it'll cost you a few hours of sleep
To sit by her side
Wrapped in a thin sheet of scratchy cotton they call a blanket
She'll tell you you to go home
"You don't have to stay here"
Though the truth is
You wouldn't know home if not for her
Tripping over memories
Childhood regrets
Spilled milk
Split chins
Sliced hair
Sitting here in the dark
It feels safe to stumble over stories
The way it looked then
Different from how it feels now
Except for outside
Wrapped in a thin sheet of snow you call a blanket
That never changes
Or does it?
Paid parking
From six to ten
Move along quickly
Don't get stuck in one place
It'll cost you the better years of your life

Sequestre Perspective

WHEN YOU VENTURE OUT

When you venture out today
Go as the crow flies
Which is meant to say
Spread your wings
Expand in the direction of the wind
Take up space. Fly.
Unencumbered by steel cages on four wheels
Telling you when to stop, go & slow down.
Limiting your direction and turning to the left
This is one way you can't enter.
She's flying high above you soaring just that way
And calling to you. Come with me.
When you venture out today
Go as the crow flies
Which is meant to say
Lift your neck high
Expand in the direction of the sun
Light the world on fire. Fly.
Unencumbered by steel masculinity on two legs
Telling you when to stop, go & kneel down.
Limiting your direction and pushing you into the ground
Because up is one way you don't belong.
She's flying high above you soaring just that way
And calling to you. Come with me.
When you venture out today
Go as the crow flies
Which is meant to say
Expand in the direction of the earth.
Become again. Fly.
Unencumbered by steel egos' on one body

Lisa Van Ahn

Telling you when to stop, go & look down.
Limiting your direction and keeping you small.
Because remembering is too much love for one person.
She's flying high above you soaring just that way
And calling to you. Come with me.
When you venture out today
Go as the crow flies
Which is meant to say
Expand in all directions.
You are the crow. Fly.
Unencumbered.
No telling where to glide, dart & hover.
Limiting nothing.
Because all directions are one.
You're flying high above soaring just that way
And calling to the next below. Come with me.

Sequestre Perspective

HEAVY VS. LIGHT

What's heavy
Your body walking with shame
Innocence lost from betrayal
Attention given with expectations
Never measuring up
What's light
Your body walking with joy
Innocence attained with vulnerability
Attention given unconditionally
Never giving less than your best today
What's heavy
Past hurts and trauma
Living your now from yesterday
Doing what they think you should do
Carrying your resentments
What's light
Past in the past
Living your now right now
Doing what you know feels right
Carrying forgiveness in your heart

Lisa Van Ahn

NEW LIFE

New life
New opportunity
New chances
New skills
New growth
New love
Comes with…
New hardship
New obstacles
New heartbreak
New struggles
New frustrations
New hurts

Sequestre Perspective

WHOLE 30 WHOLE HEARTED

Black coffee doesn't suit me well
Dark & murky
Twisted with bitterness
I long for blue skies
Lush grass
Sunny days
& clouds of cream
Sweetening the past
With a silver spoon stir
Swirling to forget
With each clink
Everything lost
Pain endured
Heart broken
Again
It's not my first attempt
I've had so many now
Black coffee doesn't suit me well
& yet I will try again

Lisa Van Ahn

START RIGHT NOW

When do you decide to live?
You can after heartache
You can after loss
You can after trauma
Or
Maybe you can start right now
After heartaches
After losses
After traumas
You can start right now

Sequestre Perspective

HOW MUCH

How much we want to love
How much we want to share

Our heartaches
Our rejections
Our traumas

Deeply we desire connection
To release

The heartaches
The rejections
The traumas

How much we want to love
How much we want to share

To be seen, witnessed, recognized

With heartaches
With rejections
With traumas

How much we build walls to prevent this release
How much we are afraid of
More heartaches
More rejections
More traumas

Lisa Van Ahn

"I love you"
How much we need these words with presence.

"Show up as you are, it is enough"

How much we crave these words.

And we curl in tightly
Hearts guarded
Afraid to speak our truth
Because
Maybe our how much
Is too much

Sequestre Perspective

SOME DAYS

There is a day, you die inside. For many reasons you die.
There is a day, you live outside. For many reasons you live.
One day you decide your insides can be your outsides.
Then you walk tall and you live free. You take it on.
Or you shrink small and you live chained. You take it on.
One day you decide your outsides can be your insides.
Then you act confidently. You pretend you can't be hurt.
Or you feel fear. You pretend it isn't real.
These are most days.
Most days your insides and outsides are your always.
You always feel outside the way you act inside.
You always feel inside the way you act outside.
Until the day you become aware.
That day becomes some days.
So some days you die inside and for many reasons you live.
And some days you live outside and for many reasons you die.
Some days you feel it all and you love it all.
And this is the reason
You are here.
Awareness,
and remembering,
to live some days…

Lisa Van Ahn

THE GREAT STATE OF BEING

Every day I wake up I work to get by
I look for a chance to prove myself
But to you it looks like the worst
No matter how hard I try
How can I measure up to your great state of being?
You do it right.
You do it first.
You do it because you don't know nothin' else.
Learned it from your father and my father tells me too
I gotta do it better than all the rest do.
How can I measure up to your great state of being?
Love tells me I will get by
But all my mistakes coupled with many great lies say
How can I measure up to your great state of being?
And being is this
It is being me
The best that I can be
Yet I never measure up to your great state of being.
Love heals. Love allows. Love wins. Love beats all.
So what if I don't measure up to your great state of being.
In truth you are being all that you have learned.
Your criticism stings
Yet it is all that you know
And how sad
Even you can't measure up to your great state of being.
Every day you wake up you work to get by.
You look for a chance to prove yourself
But to you it looks like the worst
No matter how hard you try.
So you judge harshly on my great state of being.

Sequestre Perspective

I look up.
I look ahead.
My place in this world is only half said.
There is more to come and in time you will see
My great state of being is more than you see.
And even now, right where I stand, I can say
With love, I measure up
In my great state of being.

Lisa Van Ahn

WASH YOUR HANDS

Every morning she washed her hands. There was a protocol.

First run them under the water for 12 seconds 19 times. Then put soap on them 1 time and rub her hands together for 30 seconds. Run them under the water for 3 seconds 11 times.

She'd been doing this for 4 years since October 10th. This morning she did the math. She didn't have school after all and it was easy.

Covid-19 broke out on 12/19.

It was declared to be a public health emergency of international concern on 1/30.

Then recognized as a pandemic on 3/11.

On 4/10 1.6 million cases of Covid-19 had been reported.

Now there were approximately 95,600 deaths.

She added up her hours of life. She was 10.9 yrs old. The same number of deaths that had happened in hours of her life lived.

She was a math genius. Willing to run numbers to prevent paranoia, to help her feel more calm.

Except now she knew it was all her fault. This whole thing was her fault.

Every morning she washed her hands. There was a protocol.

Sequestre Perspective

Today she stopped washing her hands. The very same day most people started her exact protocol:

First run them under the water for 12 seconds 19 times. Then put soap on them 1 time and rub your hands together for 30 seconds. Run them under the water for 3 seconds 11 times.

And, now do it for the next 4 years.
She won't. She stopped washing her hands.
Sometimes it's better to not do the math.

Lisa Van Ahn

IT BEGINS WITH A FEVER

She stared blankly at him for a moment before responding,

"Got what?"

"The virus. It's taking over everyone." Then he explained it to her.

"It begins with a fever. You want to read everything the media puts out and consume it with a fervor. The next symptom is shortness of breath.

You stop taking deep, mindful breaths, and you start to react in life with shallow ones that bring up fear and anxiety. Then you cough it all out. You cough out negativity onto everyone you see. And it's very contagious."

"Is there a remedy?"

"Yes", he said.

"It's love."

WHEN SHE JUMPED

It's not possible to want to live another day. There have been too many days in a row filled with suffering.

It's what she thought as she stood over the Hennepin Avenue bridge. She looked into the dark water on an unusually warm evening in early April.

Everything had gone sideways in less than 3 weeks. A pandemic called Covid-19 was encircling the world. Everyone was quarantined. People were required to stay home.

She was walking on a bridge. With every intention of jumping off of it.

Last night she'd lost a patient to Covid-19 and watched his entire family grieve his death through a glass wall.

Yesterday she also learned -through a phone call- that her sister, who had Covid-19, went into early labor and died during the emergency delivery procedure. She couldn't be there. All international travel was halted and she couldn't get to Italy.

These were her personal touch points which were too much to handle, but for weeks she'd been ingesting the information. Thousands of people were dying. This wasn't going to end anytime soon. Life was altered indefinitely, forever.

The last length of this plank was when she stepped out for her break from the hospital tonight.

Lisa Van Ahn

She saw a man and his daughter walking towards the hospital. He pulled at the girl's arm quickly with great force, then said,

"I can't do this with you right now, you're too much".

A flood of everything hit her in that moment and she remembered it had been too many days in a row filled with suffering since she was 5 years old.

She had 15 minutes on break. Enough for a cigarette, but she didn't smoke like a lot of the others.

It wasn't a long walk from HCMC to the Hennepin bridge. And once she was there it was eerily quiet. No cars. No bikes. No people. She was listening to her favorite Spotify playlist.

She looked into the dark water on this unusually warm evening in April.

In fact it was 65 degrees. It was going to snow on Sunday. Easter Sunday, and Passover on Thursday and all the things where people would meet and come together and they couldn't. No one could come together.
She attentively took off her key card and lanyard, her headphones, her jacket with a pen tucked into the lapel, and gently placed them on the ledge over the railing. She stepped closer to the rail almost ready to step on it.

When a brush of wind hit her. She felt some kind of magic in the air. She settled at the railing looking into the dark water. There is a place where nothing better than death exists. She'd known it and felt it before. But tonight wasn't it.

Sequestre Perspective

She turned around and walked away. Determined to rent a car and drive up to Michigan to hug her parents one last time. To tell them in person how much she loved them. To be alive and do things differently. To start fresh.

She walked away from the bridge.

Two hours later, a biker rode by the same spot noting the items she'd left and called the emergency hotline to let them know, in case someone went missing.

Maybe she'd jumped over the side.

He texted a friend,

"It was real sad to see that stuff just lying there on the cold steel above the river."

Her key card and lanyard, her headphones, her jacket with a pen tucked into the lapel, everything she'd placed so gently on the ledge over the railing, was evidence of her freedom.

She'd definitely jumped.

Lisa Van Ahn

AN ABORTION STORY

Alone in her sterile room. Only moments ago the doctor and her nurse had left her there on the table.

They were pretty nonchalant about it all.

You might have some bleeding and discomfort for a while. Expect some cramping.

"You were lucky", she thought to herself.

That was a close call and she didn't need anything attaching to her for the rest of her life.

She never wanted children. It was an instant choice.

Pro-life. Her life. It mattered to her to live it the way she wanted to live it.

All the ones out there spouting about keeping the fetuses alive were anti-choice. They didn't get what a big deal it was to bring another human into the world and handle that kind of responsibility.

Or maybe they did. And then they didn't know her. It wasn't something she was designed to do.

Never a mother. Never mothered. Never bothered, with taking care of someone else. Other than herself.
She felt her heart slow down to an almost imperceptible beat.

Sequestre Perspective

The room was quiet, bright, and hysterically white. It smelled of disinfectant.

She saw swabs on the counter, generic art on the walls, her legs still spread wide under the thin gown while she laid her head back down on the butcher paper.

Alone.

She looked at the popcorn ceiling

Alone.

No, this was less than.

Never a mother. Never mothered. Never bothered with taking care of anything.

Not even herself.

Just lonely.

Lisa Van Ahn

PERSPECTIVE

The end of the world was yesterday. She had no idea. She was living gloriously alive in a bunker in the basement of her home since the news broke.

It happened swiftly in January of 2056. Within hours, the channels of every platform of every corner of the internet were flooded with news of an alien invasion of epic proportion.

They were coming. And it couldn't be stopped. There was nowhere to go. It would happen in waves. Small parts of the world were going to be wiped out piece by piece to clear the earth of its toxicity.

All government organizations in the world had received the communication that came from a sector of space unrecognizable to them, but very clear.

'The value in this place is only salvageable by destroying humanity.'

It came in morse code. Exactly like this:

"Humans are a virus that must be obliterated in order to save earth".

How it looks in morse code most would never know but it was delivered via very clear and true channels: The News and the Government.

As soon as it hit the media she left her phone on the counter in the kitchen, walked down the stairs to her basement, opened the hidden door beyond her washer and locked herself inside.

She had enough food to last her 6 months. She needed nothing and no one. The plan, she determined, was that by the time three weeks were up the world would have been "cleared" by the invasion and she could re-enter it with plenty of open and available resources to her.

She imagined there would be a few other people like her who were smart, also hunker down. She wouldn't be the only one left. And honestly she felt like if she was, that would be alright with her.

She could be alone forever. That was just fine. No big deal.

The end of the world was yesterday. She had no idea. She was lying dead in a bunker in the basement of her home 6 months before the news broke.

Lisa Van Ahn

JUST A NUMBER

ONE.

Words aren't the truth. They are only a medium to help you hopefully connect your truth to another's truth.

The only way to connect is to connect.

Use as many different methods as you need to arrive at the truth.

You are one. A measurement of everything. Any way you attempt to split it you come back to yourself.

The only way to connect is to connect.

THE PILL WORKS IF YOU TAKE IT

It's all healing. Whether you label it pain or pleasure. It doesn't matter.

It's healing because the lesson lives inside of the feeling. You may not have the skill to witness this. It doesn't matter.

The pill works if you take it.

And spoiler alert, you took it. You catapulted yourself from the infinite oneness into this illusion of many ones.

So here you are inside of the pill. Hopefully remembering your wholeness in all of it.

Pain. Pleasure. Up, down. Inside out. Turn yourself into another and feel all of it because you ARE that.

And tomorrow when you see the carcass on the side of the freeway it's no longer roadkill hit by a moving vehicle, but rather an evolving into expansion.

Dead skin shedding itself since it no longer needs protection from hurts and traumas because all of it is glorious and one.

Lisa Van Ahn

NINE YEARS OLD

I am 9 years old.
This is what's happening tonight.
My gender doesn't matter.
My ethnicity doesn't matter.
My religion doesn't matter.
My origin doesn't matter.
This is what's happening tonight.

I am starving and haven't eaten in two days. My baby sister is crying next to me. She's starving too.

I am tucked into bed. My mom is reading the Harry Potter series to me before sleep.

I am in a locked closet. In a few hours I'll be brought into a room where I'll be raped. Over and over.

I am spending the night at my best friend's house. We're gonna play video games and eat popcorn.

I am spending the night at my grandpa's house. I don't want him to come into the room, it feels gross when he does.

I am having pizza night with my family and my little sibs. We're laughing at all the YouTube fail videos we love.

I am sitting on the corner with my mother and my brother. We're hoping to get enough cash from cars passing by to get dinner tonight.

Sequestre Perspective

I am fighting with my older sister. She doesn't respect my space. I hate her.

I am here in this "camp" and I don't know where my mom is, I haven't seen her in weeks. I keep asking when I can see her. No one tells me anything.

I am at a dance recital. I have a solo dance tonight, I feel nervous and excited for it.

I am watching my dad drink and shoot up. Soon his friends will come over and I'll try my best to hide in the closet.

I am at a charity gala for the animal humane society. I am wearing my best outfit and petting all the animals they brought to the event.

I am going to tell my parents I don't feel right in my body, I feel I am not in the right body and I am scared of how they will react.

I am playing at the park with my two besties and we're having a sleepover after a night at the movies.

I am lying in the hospital. It might be my last night here. The tube down my throat is killing me. I overheard the doctor tell my mom I didn't have long.

This is what's happening tonight.
My gender doesn't matter.

My ethnicity doesn't matter.
My religion doesn't matter.
My origin doesn't matter.
This is what's happening tonight.
And I am 9 years old.

Lisa Van Ahn

BEGIN AGAIN

"Begin Again." The words echoed in my ears.

I lived most of my childhood with an anxious tic. Every time I made a mistake I would shake my head and tell myself, "I'm starting my life over right now."

With a violent shake of my neck to the right I would try desperately to erase my entire past and start my life over with a jarring, externally obvious move.

I wanted a perfect life. No mistakes. No errors. No reminders of my faulty missteps, traumas, and glaring unworthiness.

It never worked. Instead I had concerned parents who took me to see the doctor because they couldn't figure out what was wrong with me.

Why does she make these sudden sharp head movements every 30-60 seconds?

I was undiagnosable. Maybe it was a phase. Yes, turns out it was. At some point, around-what-age-I'm-not-entirely-sure, I gave up.

I wasn't going to get better. I wasn't going to forget the traumas, I wasn't going to become cool to the kids in school, I wasn't going to be perfect, or worthy. The tic stopped. My suffering did not. Now, 20 years later I sat in excruciating silence at my Vipassana meditation retreat.

It was to my benefit to sit without moving. I fidgeted every minute or so.

It was to my benefit to release my thoughts. They continued racing through my head.

It was to my benefit to feel the sensations happening in my body and not attach to them. I couldn't stop thinking about the pain in my hip and the needles pricking at my fallen asleep crossed feet. I was very attached.

Begin again.

The words echoed in my ears.

Taking a deep breath in I repeated the words to myself. "Begin again."

Not starting my life over right now. No. Everything I'd experienced had brought me to this place. I couldn't start my life over. I was finally beginning to understand I didn't want to either.

No, with the improbability of forgetting all the pain and suffering, pretending it didn't happen or worse punishing myself for being through traumatic experiences and making unskillful choices, I knew I didn't need to erase it. I only needed to learn from it.
This phrase was a softer, gentle reminder than 'starting my life over right now'.

>You don't need to start over, dear one.

>You only need to move forward, dear one.

>And don't give up, dear one.

>Lisa Van Ahn

I believe in you, dear one.

I see you, dear one.

I am here. I love you.

Just begin again.

ROSIE

I met her on the plane. I was already sitting in the aisle seat when she threw her ginormous purse around and asked, "can I get into the window seat next to you?"

I pulled my legs in tight to my body and she jumped right over them. Two minutes later the flight attendant crossed over my seat to ask if she was actually sitting in her assigned seat.

Earbuds in, she only responded to the small touch of the flight attendant on her shoulder.

She pulled out her ear bud closest to me, and looked at the attendant.

"Excuse me, what did you say?"

"Ma'am is this your assigned seat?"

Uhhhhmm, no. It's up in 20 E (this was the row of 32 D).

"Well I'm trying to put two people seated apart together would you mind moving back to your seat?"

"Ahhhhh, nope. I need to sit in the back of the plane. That's why I'm always the last one on."

This seemed to be a true statement since I'd been on the plane for 15 minutes and no one else had gotten on the plane for awhile.

Lisa Van Ahn

She was the last person on the plane. She picked an empty seat and sat where she wanted. One seat away from me at the back of the plane.

The flight attendant looked at her with wide, confused eyes and didn't seem to know what to offer as an answer.

Then…

She lifted the ear bud hanging from the side of her body back into her ear, as if there was no more discussion to be had. That was it. She was gonna sit in the window seat in the last row of the plane.

All the confidence.

With one empty seat between us. So sure of herself. There was no other option available. Nothing to discuss.

I was sitting in the last row of the plane on the aisle. She was across one empty seat at the window and I wanted to feel as sure of myself as she did.

My name is Rosie. I'm an artist. I'm 8 years old. I can't wait to see my dad in Seattle and my mom is setting up a website for me to share my art with the world. It's not out yet, but will be soon. When I actually meet her for real I'm drawing on my sketch pad. She drags her ginormous purse over the middle seat, sitting empty between us, lodges it under her own seat, takes her right ear bud out again, and looks over at me,

"Wow, that's some great work!"

I've been drawing since I was 4 years old and it took me a long time and honestly a lot of using different artist apps on my IPad plus watching YouTube videos to learn how to draw Anime. It's the style I like to draw and I hope one day I'll be an artist.

Weirdly, I tell her all of this.

She smiles, "Girl, you're already an artist. You're doing it. And that piece you're drawing now shows amazing talent. You get to be exactly who you want to be!"

I smile, because it feels nice to have someone see how much I love being me and doing what I love. I've been living in my grey beret with glitter stars on it for more than 6 cold winter months, and no one I know wears berets. Only me.

I kinda feel like she would though. If she had one.

I'm also wearing a lace skirt and no one I know does that. I don't really fit in and I still feel kinda okay about it.

However, lately, it's been harder to make friends and be myself. I care about fitting in more than I used to. I'm not great at it and have started to worry I might be so different than everyone else.

I'm really excited to see my dad in Seattle and be with my friends out there all summer. I used to live there. My mom decided to move to Minnesota. I love her. Also, so excited to go back. And also, really nervous too.

I look left to her at the window seat and smile. She smiles back and tells me her name is Lisa.

"That's my aunt's name."

Lisa Van Ahn

She laughs and says it's so crazy but she's an aunt too. She has 12 nieces and nephews and her littlest sister has another baby coming too.

"It's gonna be lucky 13."

I can hear her music through her earbuds, but she leaves the one closest to me out of her ear, hanging in front of her, and I know it's because she wants to be able to hear me if I ask a question or want to talk to her.

She pulls a magazine out of her bag and starts to read.

I turn a page in my sketch book and look over at her again.

I start to draw.

I pencil out her face, hair, and outfit. I like her. She sits quietly reading and subtly lifts the shade on her window up. I wonder if it's because she knows I'm drawing her.

When I finish I tap her on the shoulder because she's still reading.

"I made a drawing of you."

She gushes. Not in a fake way. More like, genuine awe of my talent and also me being myself so confidently. I inhale and breathe the feeling in. It's really good.

I feel seen.

She tells me it's an honor I've drawn her. Then continues…

Sequestre Perspective

"I literally came from the frame store yesterday with 4 new pieces of art to have framed and add to my art wall. I'm going to take precious care of this and take it to the frame store too. I can't wait to put this on my art wall. I now have an original Rosie. It happened in the moment. There's no copies. It's the only one made. Ever. Do you know how much this is gonna be worth in 20 years when you're living your life as an artist?"

I stop for a second. Is she for real?

"How much?"

"Priceless. I wouldn't sell it for a million dollars."

Smile.

Quiet. Solid. I feel a little more confident. I'm pretty awesome and this has been a good trip so far.

I look out the window and notice fluffy clouds passing by Lisa's window. It's her window. She's a window girl. I'd already started to get it.

Everything she sees brings possibility. We talk a little more. She's a former fighter. Really? She's been on American Ninja Warrior. I think I've seen her and she assures me I haven't. She was cut from the show but still got accepted both times she applied.

Really? She's been in movies too, as a stunt double so I wouldn't recognize her even if I saw the movies. Really? Yup.

"Teach me your ways."

Lisa Van Ahn

She laughs out loud.

"You already got this. Stay where you're at. Be who you are. It's amazing."

I think, Really?

I tell her. It's hard out there. I get teased a lot for being so unique. I've had a lot of hurtful comments thrown my way.

She nods.
I feel like she gets it. So I continue,

"Sometimes I want to give up but my dad says it'll be okay."

"Rosie, it's often hard. You know my dad always told me 'this too shall pass' and I hated hearing it. Until one day I got it. Sometimes stuff is hard. Sometimes it's easy. Either way, it will pass. And your dad is right too, it's gonna be okay."

My nose starts bleeding. It happens to me sometimes with pressure change and when Lisa points it out I stuff a napkin up my nose and she laughs.

"I couldn't write this, " she says.

We have so many laughs about the napkin crumpled up, hanging out of my nose and how funny it is plus all the memes we could create with it (if we were gonna take pics but we're not, after all, I'm 8 yrs old and I know not to take pics with people I meet on planes) and the things we would say about it.

*napkin hanging out of the nose

Sequestre Perspective

Meme: I didn't trust gravity

*napkin hanging out of the nose

Meme: This happens all the time
*napkin hanging out of the nose

Meme: No, it's okay. I promise.

After what feels like a thousand laughs we're ready to land. It takes a while to get off the plane and when it's finally our turn to stand up she pulls her ginormous purse out from under the seat and slings it over her shoulder.

Turns back.

Smiles.

Moves on.

I shout out,

"Hey, I'm going to miss you Lisa".

Turns around.

Smiles.

Walks towards me and hands me a small pencil bag.

It's cool with pink and white writing on it and says FLY, F.L.Y., First Love Yourself all over it.

Lisa Van Ahn

"This is for you. FLY girl, First love yourself. Always. Just so you know, one of my favorite flights of all time and I've had some epic flights too.

"Really???"

It's all I can think to say, and she's already walking up the aisle and off the plane. Moving the other direction. To wherever she's going. In my mind I imagine it's someplace magical.

She probably thinks so too.

Turns back.

Smiles.

"Best flight ever."

Definitely.

ATTACHED

The sunlight streamed in the window, casting a small golden circle on the fuchsia duvet of her queen size bed. Curling up in a small ball in the middle of the bright patch she made herself as small as possible, arms squeezing her bruised knees tight into her chest and let the rolling sobs she'd been holding in all day takeover her body.

She'd spent the night on her hands and knees obsessively cleaning the floors of the space. She'd needed something to distract her from what was coming in less than 24 hours.

They were coming today to take him from her, she'd known it was happening for more than a month, but was unable to control it due to her circumstances. She felt a complete wash of shame for her inability to protect him from what was coming and what would occupy his space in the future. She was desperate, yet incapable of fixing it.

For the last 15 years he'd been her lifeline, safety, and shelter from the atrocities of the world. She'd woken up each morning, boiled some water, dropped 4 scoops into the French press and then would admire him while the brew steeped into dark richness.

She'd turn on the speaker and play a perfect song before grabbing the creamer out of the fridge, smiling at him while pouring cream into her mug. Always cream first, at least a quarter up the mug, before pouring in the coffee. Then black liquid would meld into the white and swirl together creating a genuine entwining that could never be broken.

Lisa Van Ahn

That's how she felt about him. So many of her memories were threaded with him and nothing could pull them apart. Yet here they were, being pulled apart.

She lifted her pained body up off the bed, and stepped into the hallway. Slowly, intentionally, she took everything in, one foot in front of another, walking through the memories of their time together and sliding the back pads of her finger tips fondly along the wall while she moved through the space.

The first time she'd laid eyes on him was after a small heartbreak. She'd been living in the desert in a small stucco two bedroom condo. She'd bought it with her then-boyfriend. It was at a record low price when they purchased it. Three years after sporadically living in it together, but mostly apart, they'd come to the conclusion it was best to part ways. In the split he kept the place, however, it had grown considerably in value. After the appraisal she'd moved back to her hometown with a nice chunk of change.

She was sitting on that money when she met him. He was standing close to Minnehaha park, right near the falls. She saw him from a distance and almost instantly loved him. He was strong and solid, very sure of himself. She made a move towards him and introduced herself. He quietly received her presence and smiled.

He didn't make a show of himself or put up a front. He simply was as he was. He offered himself up to her that way and they hit it off. She wasn't sure though, and he fully accepted her when she explained she'd need to play the field a bit and check out some other options. She did, knowing she'd been attracted to him instantly she still messed around with other options for a month or two. Everyday her thoughts kept drifting back to him and their first meeting near the falls.

She knew where to find him so she went. He'd waited patiently for her and when she arrived he was there with a knowing energy. They were meant for each other from the beginning. He hadn't been anxious in any way. He knew she'd come back to start a life with him. She was in awe. He'd never wavered in his belief of her, so sure of himself. She was sold, totally in love.

There was a deep, audible sigh and it startled her out of her memories.

She giggled slightly. It wasn't him. "But it might've been", she thought to herself. Her own breath had become heavy again. She felt tears and didn't want him to see. She moved into the living room shaking with emotion.

Even though it was so hard, it was marked for her to spend these last moments together before they took him away.

Lowering herself to the floor, she placed her cheek on the cold vinyl, and spread out her arms and legs wide. When she'd met him for the second time, in this exact spot, so many years ago, it had been carpet. They made a life together for two happy years here, but she left him for a while.

When she left, she believed it was out of necessity. They were content, just the two of them, but she met another and requested to bring this other into the relationship. He agreed to it. The other agreed to it too. She loved having both of them in her life. Everything felt full and perfect. However, the other wasn't as much of a fan of him and wanted to move on. Then the other became insistent about leaving him behind, and convinced her to pack up and go. She did.

Lisa Van Ahn

She would check in every once in a while with him. For seven years she'd occasionally pop over and see how he was and always, always, he assured her that he loved her and would be there for her if she ever decided to come back.

At the end of the seventh year things with the other had unraveled so completely she didn't have anywhere to go. The other was done with her and though he graciously offered her a place to live she could feel his apathy and bitterness permeate into the marrow of her bones. She knew too, the other had always resented him.
Over the years they'd had so many conversations about how she should let him go, cut ties completely, just be done with him.

She packed a suitcase, put a few things in her car, and headed back to him, happy she'd never let him go completely. And she thought she never would. He welcomed her back with open arms. She knew she was home with him and grateful for his steadfast love even in her betrayal.

Now, in the present moment, her belly rose and fell on the flooring. She turned her cheek to the other side and it wasn't cold any longer, warmed from having the left side of her face there for more than five minutes. She could feel him watching her lying spread eagle on the floor.

It was when she left the other and moved back in with him that the carpet had been ripped out and the beautiful vinyl flooring was installed. It looked like hardwood, and was a light shade of grey, with the appearance of wood grain. It brightened up the place considerably. There'd also been a fresh coat of paint too. For a short time, while she was with the other, he had invited a woman into his life. He didn't love the woman and knew she was a temporary, albeit needed, replacement to her.

Sequestre Perspective

He graciously allowed the woman in and silently let her smoke in the house even though he detested it. When she moved back in they freshened the space up together replacing the other woman's scent of stale smoke and ignorance with brand new everything.

They were happy again. And had been. For a time. Then last year she lost her job. It had been rough. She took odd cleaning jobs, and desperately tried to make ends meet. Each night she'd come home to him and he'd hold her and comfort her. He appreciated her effort and gave her security. Sometimes things don't last, she thought. Security is an illusion, this proves it.

She knew it was time, they were coming for him at 3pm today and it was nearly 2:45pm. She'd cleared everything out of the space already, well almost. The bed was still in there and made up. It had been important to her for them to spend their last night together in comfort. There was also one suitcase sitting outside the front door.

She wanted to wait until the last possible moment to say goodbye to him. She stood up from the floor lost in the memories of love she'd experienced with him. Her body began to shake as she got closer to their final goodbye.

Then abruptly there was a knock at the front door.

She wanted to wait until the last possible moment to say goodbye to him. She stood up from the floor lost in the memories of love she'd experienced with him. Her body began to shake as she got closer to their final goodbye.

Then abruptly there was a knock at the front door.

They were here. Early. Her stomach dropped. It was time. She walked into the kitchen and looked at him with a panic. Please don't

Lisa Van Ahn

make me say goodbye. I don't want to leave you. I need you. I love you. Please. Please. Please.
The knock came again louder and stronger this time with voices yelling at her from the other side. She walked slowly to it, turned the deadbolt, and opened it. On the other side stood two officers in uniform. They stated her name two times, and then…

"Is this you?

"Yes it is."

"Ma'am, this is an order of immediate eviction. You received a judicial order of foreclosure on this property 30 days ago and haven't paid your back mortgage. We are here to make sure you exit the property right now."

"I've been trying, I just don't have all the money together."

"Ma'am, that isn't our problem. You need to leave now."

"I know."

She turned and took one more look at him. Empty, quiet, and void of the love they had created together, she took a deep breath in and on the exhale silently said to him,

"I love you so much. I will never forget you."

She stepped around the officers as they walked in to occupy him. She picked up her suitcase, walked up the stairs, and out the front door. At the street she turned and looked at his exterior. She started to feel everything. Just everything.

Sequestre Perspective

The exterior of her heart hardened, and in one moment she built an indestructible damn, unwilling to let the feelings flow. She retracted from the pain and jammed it deep inside as far down into her as she could. She straightened her face, grit down on her teeth, and locked up her body.

With a fraudulent shrug, she said to herself, "it's just a house." She turned away from him, missing the tears falling from the stucco.

Lisa Van Ahn

THE CONTAINER

She'd always lived next to the dock. And for years her dad worked the docks.

She would wake up well before dawn with him and take the short 3 block walk down to the port where all the shipping containers lived.

He would tell her to sit quietly in the booth and play her video games while he'd walk the walls of shipping containers working security.

She used to do as she was told. Even though it wasn't her style. But two months ago, things changed.

She stopped sitting quietly.

It wasn't her style, anyway.

As soon as he was out of sight she'd sneak out of the booth and begin on the opposite end he traveled.

Her father was a perfectionist. He had a method to his rounds and he would start on the south end, moving west, and turning each corner moving easy and rounding down to the north end.

She knew this.

So she would begin at the north end, run down to the east side, and move south.

She knew she had at least 20 minutes before she would run into him.

Sequestre Perspective

There were miles of shipping containers in the docks and she wanted to check all of them.

She had a feeling about it.

As much as her dad was a perfectionist she knew he didn't take his job with purpose. It was a paycheck. Something to help fund his family. her and two younger sisters who were still in diapers.

He needed to provide for his family and it was just a job.

For her, it was a mission.

Anna was 15 years old. Smarter than her years. Not interested in the day-to-day drama happening at her school. She felt there was something bigger she was meant to do in the world.

She read a lot online, and 2 months ago she'd read an article about a sex ring that was captured after a young girl escaped from a shipping container in England. It wasn't in a port city like hers, she lived in Denmark, but she re-lived the story daily knowing where her father worked.

She was confident that not every shipping container in the port held goods and merchandise that weren't human. After reading that article she'd made it her daily purpose in life to check every container.

So for 2 months she'd been practicing this routine.

Her father would leave, she would wait, then she would go the opposite direction checking each container.

Lisa Van Ahn

She had a very solid method. She'd knock lightly on each container and say quietly in the two languages she knew,

Are you okay? I'm friendly. (English)

Har du det godt? Jeg er venlig. (Danish)

She would wait for a moment and listen for any rustling. If nothing she would move to the next container and methodically repeat her system.

She'd been checking containers for 2 months and felt relieved every time there was no reply. She'd almost started to believe that her port, the port of her city was impervious to human slavery.
After all, every person she encountered was lovely and pleasant.

Tonight was a full moon. She stopped to enjoy it. She also thought maybe tonight would be her last night checking containers. She felt secure in her father's work, she felt secure in the integrity of her city.

She felt like maybe she could start sleeping soundly in her bed knowing nothing tragic was happening at the docks close to her home.

As she looked happily at the moon she felt grateful for her loving father and her sisters and mother. And then she heard a small whimper.

She quickly turned and saw a young girl, covered in bruises and blood.

"My dear, oh my dear, let me help you".

Sequestre Perspective

She ran to the young girl, and as she moved forward, the girl retracted.

"Oh no, it's okay. I'm so sorry, I won't hurt you I promise".

The girl cautiously moved towards her, Anna reached out a hand, as you might for a nervous, stray animal. She waited there with her palm face up, not moving.

Silent.

After a few moments the young girl moved closer. Since Anna wasn't sure how to communicate with her, she spoke in English first.
"What container did you come from? I will help you get out of here."

The young girl didn't seem to understand so she asked in Danish. The girl's answer was astonishing.

"Jeg kom ikke fra en container. Jeg kom fra lageret."

Anna moved quickly.

She knew it was important. Even though it would implicate her father. And in that most important moment, she had a fleeting thought, wondering if it was possible he could be a part of it all as well.

Her fleeting thought quickly became a knowing horror.

He always told of his break times in the warehouse, bullshitting with his buddies, playing games after things were quiet, and the security checks were done.

Lisa Van Ahn

The warehouse was a safe space for him and his guys.

Away from his daughter knocking on container doors looking for pain and suffering.

A way for him to inflict his pain and suffering on others.

Anna grabbed her by the hand and ran into the dark with her.

She didn't know what else to do.

She had at least 15 minutes before he came back.

The girl's words rang in her ears.

"I didn't come from a container, I came from the warehouse."

ELLA DIES

Ella sat on the stoop of her building and smoked a cigarette.

It had been months since she'd picked up a pack of American Spirits at the gas station but tonight she was on edge.

She'd been on edge for a few days. She couldn't shake the feeling that someone was orchestrating her death.

Yesterday she'd gone to therapy and shared all about it with Tom. He'd been seeing her since she got out of the hospital last month.

It was part of her treatment plan to see him three times a week.

He was nice enough. Quiet and inquisitive, seemingly non-judgmental, though he would raise his eyebrows slightly when Ella told him about the person who was planning her death.

It was the entire reason she'd ended up in the psych ward anyway. They wouldn't let her out until she agreed she was delusional.

And then she had to see Tom weekly to prove she was okay.

Sitting on the stoop things didn't feel okay. There'd been so much construction around her place and getting to work every day meant she had to take new paths to arrive there. Ella didn't like going down new paths.

She liked her routines and she didn't approve of being taken out of a comfortable place. A comfortable place like taking 28th all the way down to Broad Street and turning left into her office.

Lisa Van Ahn

She crushed her cigarette and lit another thinking about the path to work she had driven earlier in the day.

She could usually just drive down 28th but because of all the road work she was detoured down Elliot Avenue, up to Larch and then Lincoln, finally it brought her down Aster Road and she was finally able to get back on 28th.

It all felt composed in some way, and there was something she couldn't put her finger on about all of it.

More than anything she hated taking the freeway, too many cars close to her driving past, but tonight she was considering taking the freeway tomorrow instead of following these detours.

She crushed out her second cigarette and went to bed feeling uneasy.

Ella had dealt with unstable emotions and anxiety for most of her life. She was aware that some of it was self-created and also had a feeling of knowing that her life was unusual and someone had been watching her for a long time waiting to kill her. She didn't know who it was and the thought was an obsession. It wouldn't leave her.

She rolled restlessly in her bed and dreamt of driving in her car, getting in a crash and not being able to exit the vehicle while it burst into flames.

At 6am she woke from her fitful night of sleep and put a pot of water on the stove to make a French press. She was still thinking she might take the freeway today.

Her coffee did little to ease her nerves. Mostly it aggravated them. She sat and watched the sun come up while she drank it and couldn't help thinking today…it happens today.

Sequestre Perspective

She left early knowing it would take longer with the detours and she made a final decision to go with them rather than taking the freeway. Shortly after hitting 28th the first road block came. Elliot, to Larch, to Lincoln, to Aster.

Today Aster was closed off to 28th since new construction had started and she went down Dowling Avenue turning right at Isle Parkway, moving left to Emerson Avenue then right on Stanford Street. It would eventually lead her to 28th, back towards work.

It took all of two seconds after taking a right on Stanford before her left brain kicked into gear and got it. She couldn't believe she hadn't seen it earlier. It was an acronym of her future.

Elliot Avenue

Larch Avenue

Lincoln Avenue

Aster Road

Dowling Avenue

Isle Parkway

Emerson Avenue

Stanford Street

E.L.L.A.D.I.E.S.

The first letters of each street she was forced down pronounced her death. Ella dies.

Lisa Van Ahn

She quickly detoured off Stanford and went straight down 28th to Tom's office instead of going to her work.

He had to know she wasn't crazy. He had to know that she knew this was coming and she wasn't delusional.

In a frenzy she parked sideways outside his small office and ran in. He was standing there and turned to look at her while she spilled her awareness onto him in a rambling tale of detours, arranged plans for her death, and told him she wasn't crazy.

He raised his eyebrows slightly and said,

"Yes, and today is the 28th of the month".

His knife went swift and deep into Ella's heart.

She was right all along.

A WISH FOR A SCAR

Marla looked in the mirror. Her eyes lingered over tired, drawn features before touching the ugly, raised streak across her neck. It had been four months and the revolting scar lived as a visible reminder of her violation. She doubted it would ever fade.

On this sunny Monday morning her thoughts pointed to the fast advancing 2pm appointment with her therapist, Riley Peters. It wasn't going to go well. She could feel it. For eight weeks she'd been seeing Riley and the sessions were a torturous hour of hopeless hypnosis, frequent tears, and probing questions that led to zero answers.

Marla wrapped a scarf around her neck, as she'd become accustomed to doing. This one was a silk, beige print with charcoal colored cat profiles printed on it. It reminded her of recently losing Jack, her cat, and as she tied it a tear welled in the corner of her lower lid. The softness of the scarf was like the silkiness of his fur. More tears surfaced and Marla let them come. There'd been so many tears in the last four months but the pain hadn't subsided.

She took a second look in the mirror; scarf wrapped around her neck, recalling that horrific night. All she could feel was the cruel blade against her skin. He'd climbed up the fire escape steps outside of her building. The smallest crack in her window was enough invitation.

There had been a cool breeze and Marla wrapped herself in only a thin, cotton sheet leaving the window slightly ajar so she could feel the wind brush across her body. After two weeks of oppressive heat in the city, the airiness of this night felt heavenly. She lay diagonally

Lisa Van Ahn

across her queen bed with the breeze sifting in through the window, drifting sweetly to sleep.

Marla didn't wake to the knife cutting the screen. It wasn't until he was on top of her forcefully pushing her onto her back and digging it into her neck that she came out of her dreams.

Her loving cat, Jack, played center stage in the dream. They were messing around together and she'd crumpled up a small ball of paper, thrown it, and he retrieved it to have her throw again. She was laughing, about to throw it again, when she was ripped awake.

Steel on her neck. A low, raspy voice that said, "Open your legs bitch."

She inhaled sharply. Wait, was this really happening?

He pushed the knife tighter to her throat and she released a small squeak. "I said, open your legs."

Instead, Marla closed them tight. She would not give anything. She would not allow this. His knife sliced deep into her throat and slid firmly past her jugular. Then as suddenly as he'd appeared he was gone.
Blood was streaming freely from her neck. She grabbed a t-shirt and pushed it firmly to her throat before reaching out for her phone and desperately calling 911. Then she blacked out.

Marla arrived for her 2pm appointment a few minutes late. Her therapist was waiting and immediately commented on her silk scarf. "So pretty Marla. Are you loving it or covering something up?"

Marla ignored her and sank into the awkwardly, overstuffed chair adjacent from Riley letting out a frustrated sigh.

Sequestre Perspective

"So, how was your weekend?" Riley offered as an introduction.

"I'm exhausted."

"Tell me more about that…"

Riley always wanted to know 'more about that', whatever it was, and Marla was never thrilled to share it. She crossed her arms and pursed her lips. Her heart wasn't willing to brave the emotional rapids today.

Riley wouldn't be discouraged. "So instead, tell me about the scarf you're wearing today, Marla."

The silk scarf; it reminded her of Jack. She looked towards Riley and hesitated. Tears began to spill from her eyes and she couldn't contain the pain. Her mouth betrayed her heart and words spilled out.

"I miss him. I miss Jack. He was my heart for nearly 17 years. I have loved him since he was a kitten. He's been with me, a part of me, for more than half of my life. I'm lost without him."

"What happened to Jack, Marla?"

"He got sick and he died. I miss him so much." The tears were streaming down her face into her lap.

Riley cautiously eased in more to the conversation. "Do you remember how he got sick?"

Marla shook her head no. She couldn't. All she remembered is that her heart hurt missing Jack's sweet spirit in her life.

Lisa Van Ahn

Riley leaned in closer. "Marla…Can you please take off your scarf today?" She'd asked her to do this so many times and it was too much, but today Marla slowly unwound the scarf to wipe the tears from her eyes and laid it in her lap.

"Touch your neck my dear. Tell me what you feel."

Marla reached up to touch the protruding scar but felt nothing, only smoothness. The look of shock on her face prompted Riley into a new question.
"Now do you remember what happened?"

Marla winced. Something was flooding in but she didn't like it. She didn't want it to be the truth. She clawed her neck searching for any reminder of the scar.

"No. I stood up for myself. I closed my legs. I wouldn't let him rape me. I said no so he slit my throat instead. That's what happened. That's what happened." She squeezed her eyes as tight as she could to create a dam and block the memories from rushing in.

Riley reached forward and held her shoulders. "You said no. You stood up for yourself. You were protecting yourself."

Marla's dam broke as everything flashed again.

Steel on her neck. A low, raspy voice that said, "Open your legs bitch."

She inhaled sharply. Wait, was this really happening?

He pushed the knife tighter to her throat and she released a small squeak. "I said, open your legs."

Sequestre Perspective

Instead, Marla closed them tight. She would not give anything. She would not allow this.

He got off of her and grabbed Jack, her cat. His knife sliced deep into Jack's throat and slid firmly past his jugular.
He climbed back on Marla and straddled her body, "If you don't want that to happen to you, spread your legs bitch." She involuntarily opened them while he raped her. Then as suddenly as he'd appeared he was gone.

Blood was streaming freely from Jack's neck. She grabbed a t-shirt and pushed it firmly to her sweet cat's throat before reaching out for her phone and desperately calling 911. Then she blacked out.

"Are you okay? Marla…Are you okay?" Riley was still holding her shoulders.

Marla's whole body shook, her vision blurred, and her head felt fuzzy. She lifted the scarf off her lap and wrapped the silk cat pattern three times around her neck.

Abruptly, she had a memory of her mama tucking her into bed, the smallest version of Jack nestled close to her, reciting a poem to ease her to sleep.

'Star light, Star bright,

First star I see tonight,

I wish I may, I wish I might,

Have this wish I wish tonight.'

Marla wished for a scar.

Lisa Van Ahn

THE ENORMITY OF LIFE

*It's 4:15am on July 26th 2019.

Margo tosses in bed and throws the covers off her naked body.

She can't sleep. Can't get the feeling out of her that she's never really done much in this world to make a difference. Can't stop the pain screaming in her left wrist. Broken and swollen, in a splint, she knows it will be fixed in surgery in a few hours. Right now though, she wonders. Is there a way to fix this meaningless wheel of life she's been spinning on?

Three miles away Lacey tosses her covers off too. She can't sleep either. And she feels sick. She cries out to her mom who comes running in seconds later,

"What's wrong honey?"

"I think I'm gonna throw up."

Mom takes her into the bathroom and pulls back her soft blonde hair taking gentle care to watch her splinted, broken wrist, and not jar it against anything.

Lacey cries while she releases the contents of last night's dinner into the toilet.

Mom rubs her back gently.

"It's gonna be okay sweetie."

Sequestre Perspective

*It's 5 am on July 26th 2019.

Margo gets up and starts her shower. She places a bag over the splinted wrist and wraps tape around it before stepping over the porcelain ledge and letting the coolish water fall over her body. She still feels listless and insignificant. A few tears fall with the water. She's not due for surgery until 7am but it seems pointless to delay any longer so after the shower she packs her bag, insurance card, ID, and calls a Lyft to take her to the hospital.

Lacey's mom draws a bath. They're due for surgery shortly and still it's important that her daughter feel loved and cared for and if they're late, well, they're late. The hospital can deal with it.
She lifts her 9-yr old daughter into the tub and gently washes her while she sings "You are my sunshine" and Lacey seems calmer. She kisses her on the forehead and then…

"Mom, am I going to be okay? I'm scared about surgery today."

"My love, yes. You will. They are going to fix your wrist up and you'll be better very soon. It's also okay to be scared."

Lacey ducks under the water holding her splinted hand up above it and blows a few bubbles.

*It's 6:15am on July 26th 2019.

Margo steps into the hospital lobby and walks towards registration. She's very early. Her surgery isn't due until 10am.

No matter. Tossing restlessly alone in her room seemed a more tragic circumstance than sitting in a waiting room for a few extra hours.

Lisa Van Ahn

As it turns out the attendant at the desk informs her there's been a delay with another patient so they can get Margo in early since she's here.

Lacey's mom calls the hospital to let them know they'll be late.

Lacey has been anxious and it's caused stomach problems for her.

She's been vomiting and needs to stabilize before coming in for surgery.

As it turns out the attendant on the phone informs her there's been an early arrival of another patient so they can take Lacey for surgery later in the day.

*It's 7:45am on July 26th 2019. Dr. Brennan has been struggling since 4:15am.

She woke with a massive migraine which never happens.

At 5am she took 2 Tylenol which she never takes.

At 6:15am she checked in for her first surgery of the day. It was meant to be a 9-year old girl, broken distal radius to implant a plate and 6 screws. Due to hiccups in scheduling she was currently reviewing what was meant to be her second surgery of the day. A 44-year old woman with a comminuted fracture requiring a plate and 9 screws.

Now she was still dealing with a splitting pain in her head while washing her hands and prepping for surgery.

Margo is alone in the hospital room. The anesthesiologist came in and explained the medication they would be using and asked if she had someone to pick her up after surgery. Yes. She said. Her sister would be coming to take her home. But, alone in the room she feels the enormity of life. What has she made of it? Where had she stayed small and not played for a purpose. And why does she feel she's never given enough? In a short time the nurses sweep in and pull up the sides of her hospital bed. The medication is inserted into the IV and she's pushed down the hallway of the hospital, she's out before she enters the operating room.

Lacey and her mom valet the car at the hospital. They take the elevator up to the third floor and move towards registration.
"Hi, well this worked out well. We've had someone else take your place in surgery and you'll be able to take their later slot. We just need you to fill out these forms and bring them back to us and we'll get you set up in a room shortly."

*It's 8:15am on July 26th 2019.

Dr. Brennan makes the incision into Margo's left wrist and feels a sharp pain in her neck at the same time. She lurches quickly and her knife slips into the radial artery as she collapses on top of Margo. The surgery staff acts quickly. Within minutes they are working to resuscitate the surgeon, stop Margo's bleeding, and calling all emergency staff into the room.

Lacey and her mom are aware there's something wrong. The hospital alarms are going off and people are running back and forth frantically. Lacey feels a small swell in her heart. And then a quiet voice. It's not her voice, but a sweet one who says,

Lisa Van Ahn

"You're going to be perfect, love. Do something wonderful and brilliant with your life. Be purposeful and make every moment matter. This moment mattered for me, and I'm glad I could give it to you. It made my life mean everything."

Margo's spirit passed through Lacey's body as she left.

A LOVE LETTER

The fight is over Dear One.

When you attach to sensation you will have suffering. But when you welcome all sensations whether they are pleasure or pain you will fall into the oneness of who you are.

You do not need to fight ever again. Whatever comes remember this; you can invite it with open arms. You can trust the process. Dear One, you are so deserving of this lesson of ease.

You've traveled many dark roads and you've done the hard work. This is your reward. So remember it gets to be easy. It always can be.

See, even when the pain comes you welcome it. And when the pleasure comes you enjoy it without wishing it to stay.

When you welcome all sensation you're in perfect equanimity and so in this place all energy moves through you effortlessly.

In no way do you resist or try to hold on. You simply let it flow through. Around you. Into and out of you.

This absence of resistance means you have no container so you can not become too full or ever be too empty.

You can hold all the pain of the world and all the pleasure of the world simultaneously and with no effort.

It's that easy and it gets to be this easy from now on.

Lisa Van Ahn

Until you forget and it becomes hard again. And when you do, I'll always be here to remind you of the perfect paradox.

This is so much work, and it's so easy.

BECAUSE OF WINTER

She didn't want to die.

But she took the pills. One after another. She didn't know how to swallow more than one at a time. She took 108 of them. One. Then a swallow of orange juice. And then another. One. 108 times. One at a time. Until death was closer.

It was enough to die.

She didn't want to though, not really.

She wanted to feel alive.

She passed out after making a call to her best friend who called 911. It was necessary. She would've died without that call.

Without support we die.

Without love we are able to breathe and exist. We can't really live though. Not live in the sense of feeling alive, only in the sense of living, scientifically.

She was breathing. She was living. And she wasn't alive. She was a zombie.

She wanted to feel alive.

She woke up in the hospital with a scratchy throat and pain through her entire body. They'd given her NarCan to reverse the effects of the pills. She'd been given charcoal, and had her stomach pumped.

Lisa Van Ahn

The feeling was unpleasant. Somehow, she felt alive.

It was 3 months and 18 days there. Staying in the hospital. Walking amongst the other zombies. Everyone breathing, existing, and not really living. She was inside for 108 days.

And she got out on 9/11.

The same day the towers crumbled and everyone out there in the US decided to feel grateful for being alive. Because of tragedy. Because of pain. Because of urgency. Because of the awareness of mortality.

She did too.

She called up her friend and thanked her for making the emergency call. She felt better about life, somehow.

She wasn't sure how, but she did and her friend invited her to a yoga class. celebrating the fall equinox. The coming of winter, generally speaking the hardest time of the year for her. All proceeds would benefit the emergency responders of 9/11.

Without support we die.
And winter was coming.
The hardest time of the year for her.

She went to the class. They did 108 salutations to the sun. 108 times. One. Then a deep breath. And then another. One. 108 times. One at a time. Until feeling alive was closer.

It was enough to live. Because the sun will always come out again. Even after the harshest winter.

She felt alive.

Sequestre Perspective

And she knew.

It wasn't in spite of, but because of, winter.

Lisa Van Ahn

ABOUT THE AUTHOR

This is being self-published and I refuse to write about myself in third person. I do not have an agent. I do not have a publisher. I have me. All of these words are mine and they may or may not interest you. That is of no consequence. I needed to write these words for me so I did. I hope you enjoy them, if you don't that is okay too..

Words have fueled and formed me since my beginning. I love reading other people's perspectives on life, how they feel, think, and choose to see it gives me a lot of joy. I believe we're all in this together and I'd love to connect. If you have words you'd like to share with me, I'd love to read them. My email is lisa@lisavanahn.com

Be well, LVA-

www.ingramcontent.com/pod-product-compliance
Lightning Source LLC
Chambersburg PA
CBHW071422070526
44578CB00003B/662